W9-DDB-302

MOORESVILLE PUBLIC LIBRARY
220 W. HARRISON ST.
MOORESVILLE, IN 46158
317 – 831 – 7323

DISCARD

MOROCCO

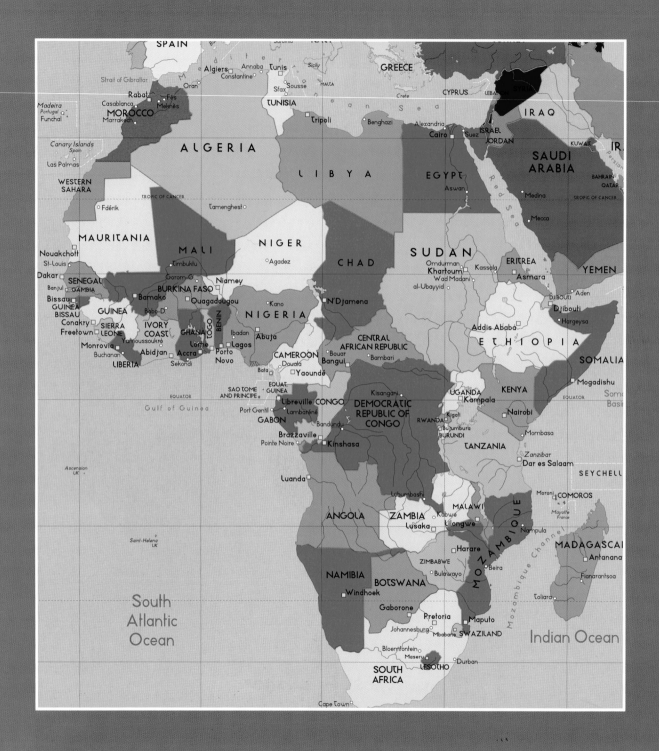

MOROCCO

Dorothy Kavanaugh

Mason Crest Publishers
Philadelphia

MAR 1 8 2008

MOORESVILLE PUBLIC LIBRARY
220 WEST HARRISON STREET
MOORESVILLE, INDIANA 46158

Produced by OTTN Publishing, Stockton, N.J.

Mason Crest Publishers
370 Reed Road
Broomall, PA 19008
www.masoncrest.com

Copyright © 2008 by Mason Crest Publishers. All rights reserved.
Printed and bound in Malaysia.

First printing

1 3 5 7 9 8 6 4 2

Library of Congress Cataloging-in-Publication Data

Kavanaugh, Dorothy, 1969-
  Morocco / Dorothy Kavanaugh.
      p. cm. — (Africa)
  Includes bibliographical references and index.
  ISBN-13: 978-1-4222-0084-1
  ISBN-10: 1-4222-0084-1
  1. Morocco. I. Title. II. Series.
  DT305.K23 2007
  964—dc22
                                        2006017339

Africa: Facts and Figures	Egypt	Nigeria
The African Union	Ethiopia	Rwanda
Algeria	Ghana	Senegal
Angola	Ivory Coast	Sierra Leone
Botswana	Kenya	South Africa
Burundi	Liberia	Sudan
Cameroon	Libya	Tanzania
Democratic Republic	Morocco	Uganda
of the Congo	Mozambique	Zimbabwe

Table of Contents

Africa: Continent in the Balance

Robert I. Rotberg

Africa is the cradle of humankind, but for millennia it was off the familiar, beaten path of global commerce and discovery. Its many peoples therefore developed largely apart from the diffusion of modern knowledge and the spread of technological innovation until the 17th through 19th centuries. With the coming to Africa of the book, the wheel, the hoe, and the modern rifle and cannon, foreigners also brought the vastly destructive transatlantic slave trade, oppression, discrimination, and onerous colonial rule. Emerging from that crucible of European rule, Africans created nationalistic movements and then claimed their numerous national independences in the 1960s. The result is the world's largest continental assembly of new countries.

There are 53 members of the African Union, a regional political grouping, and 48 of those nations lie south of the Sahara. Fifteen of them, including mighty Ethiopia, are landlocked, making international trade and economic growth that much more arduous and expensive. Access to navigable rivers is limited, natural harbors are few, soils are poor and thin, several countries largely consist of miles and miles of sand, and tropical diseases have sapped the strength and productivity of innumerable millions. Being landlocked, having few resources (although countries along Africa's west coast have tapped into deep offshore petroleum and gas reservoirs), and being beset by malaria, tuberculosis, schistosomiasis, AIDS, and many other maladies has kept much of Africa poor for centuries.

Thirty-five of the world's 50 poorest countries are African. Hunger is common. So is rapid deforestation and desertification. Unemployment rates are often over 50 percent, for jobs are few—even in agriculture. Where Africa once was a land of small villages and a few large cities, with almost everyone

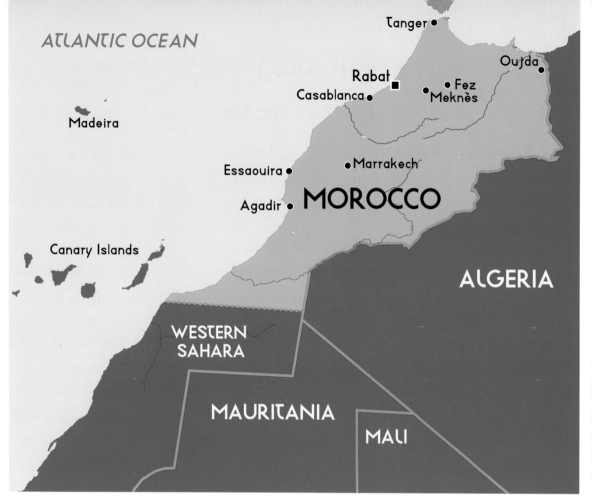

engaged in growing grain or root crops or grazing cattle, camels, sheep, and goats, today more than half of all the more than 900 million Africans, especially those who live south of the Sahara, reside in towns and cities. Traditional agriculture hardly pays, and a number of countries in Africa—particularly the smaller and more fragile ones—can no longer feed themselves.

There is not one Africa, for the continent is full of contradictions and variety. Of the 750 million people living south of the Sahara, at least 130 million live in Nigeria, 74 million in Ethiopia, 62 million in the Democratic Republic of the Congo, and 44 million in South Africa. By contrast, tiny Djibouti and Equatorial

The Berber village of Ait Benhaddou is constructed of mud bricks.

Guinea have fewer than 1 million people each, and prosperous Botswana and Namibia each are under 2.5 million in population. Within some countries, even medium-sized ones like Zambia (11.5 million), there are a plethora of distinct ethnic groups speaking separate languages. Zambia, typical with its multitude of competing entities, has 70 such peoples, roughly broken down into four language and cultural zones. Three of those languages jostle with English for primacy.

Given the kaleidoscopic quality of African culture and deep-grained poverty, it is no wonder that Africa has developed economically and politically less rapidly than other regions. Since independence from colonial rule, weak governance has also plagued Africa and contributed significantly to the widespread poverty of its peoples. Only Botswana and offshore Mauritius have been governed democratically without interruption since independence. Both are among Africa's wealthiest countries, too, thanks to the steady application of good governance.

Aside from those two nations, and South Africa, Africa has been a continent of coups since 1960, with massive and oil-rich Nigeria suffering incessant periods of harsh, corrupt, autocratic military rule. Nearly every other country on or around the continent, small and large, has been plagued by similar bouts of instability and dictatorial rule. In the 1970s and 1980s Idi Amin ruled Uganda capriciously and Jean-Bedel Bokassa proclaimed himself emperor of the Central African Republic. Macias Nguema of Equatorial Guinea was another in that same mold. More recently Daniel arap Moi held Kenya in thrall and Robert Mugabe has imposed himself on once-prosperous Zimbabwe. In both of those cases, as in the case of the late Gnassingbe Eyadema in Togo and Mobutu Sese Seko in Congo, these presidents stole wildly and drove entire peoples and their nations into penury. Corruption is common in Africa, and so are weak rule-of-law frameworks, misplaced development, high expenditures on soldiers and low expenditures on health and education, and a widespread (but not universal) refusal on the part of leaders to work well for their followers and citizens.

Conflict between groups within countries has also been common in Africa. More than 15 million Africans have been killed in the civil wars of Africa since 1990, with more than 3 million losing their lives in Congo and more than 2 million in the Sudan. Since 2003, according to the United Nations, more than 200,000 people have been killed in an ethnic-cleansing rampage in Sudan's Darfur region. In 2007, major civil wars and other serious conflicts persisted in Burundi, the Central African Republic, Chad, the Democratic Republic of the Congo, Ivory Coast, Sudan (in addition to the mayhem in Darfur), Uganda, and Zimbabwe.

Despite such dangers, despotism, and decay, Africa is improving. Botswana and Mauritius, now joined by South Africa, Senegal, and Ghana, are beacons of democratic growth and enlightened rule. Uganda and Senegal are taking the lead in combating and reducing the spread of AIDS, and others are following. There are serious signs of the kinds of progressive economic policy changes that might lead to prosperity for more of Africa's peoples. The trajectory in Africa is positive.

Morocco offers breathtaking landscapes. (Opposite) The Cascades d'Ouzoud in Tanaghmeilt is the most famous waterfall in Morocco. Ouzoud is the Berber word for "olive" and refers to the olive trees that cover the pathway to the bottom of the falls. (Right) The rocky cliffs of Morocco meet the Atlantic Ocean.

1 One Land, Many Natural Environments

MOROCCO IS LOCATED ON THE NORTHWEST CORNER of the vast African continent. It is closer to Europe than any other African country, being approximately 8 miles (13 kilometers) from Spain across the Strait of Gibraltar. The Strait of Gibraltar is the *demarcation* between Morocco's two coasts: east of Gibraltar is the Mediterranean coast. To the west and south is the Atlantic. Morocco is bordered by Algeria to the south and east. To the southwest is the disputed Western Sahara territory, which has been occupied by Moroccan troops since 1975.

With 172,413 square miles (446,550 sq km) of territory, Morocco is slightly larger than California. From sandy beaches and rugged mountains to lush forests and dry desert, Morocco is home to many varied environments.

Quick Facts: The Geography of Morocco

Location: northern Africa, bordering the North Atlantic Ocean and the Mediterranean Sea, between Algeria and Western Sahara

Area: (slightly larger than California)
  total: 172,413 square miles (446,550 sq km)
  land: 172,316 square miles (446,300 sq km)
  water: 97 square miles (250 sq km)

Borders: Algeria, 969 miles (1,559 km); Western Sahara, 275 miles (443 km); Spain, 9.9 miles (15.9 km)—Ceuta: 3.9 miles (6.3 km); Melilla: 6 miles (9.6 km); coastline, 1,140 miles (1, 835 km)

Climate: Mediterranean, becoming more extreme in the interior

Terrain: extensive plateaus, valleys, and rich lowland coastal plains border mountainous northern coast and interior; the occupied Western Sahara is mainly low, flat desert; the sandy, rocky terrain rises to small mountains in the northeast and south

Elevation extremes:
  lowest point: Sebkha Tah, 180 feet (55 m) below sea level
  highest point: Jebel Toubkal, 13,665 feet (4,165 m)

Natural hazards: northern mountains geologically unstable and subject to earthquakes; periodic droughts

Source: CIA World Factbook, 2007.

Coastal Lowlands

The broad coastal lowlands, called the Taza Depression, extend south along the Atlantic coast from Tangier to Essaouira. The flat coast, covered with sand dunes and marshes, has few natural harbors. Inland from this low area, the land slowly rises to form a large, open, irregular *plateau* that covers thousands of square miles. The plateau sits at elevations between 1,770 and 2,950 feet (540 and 900 meters) before giving way to mountains. The soil is poor, but some areas on the plateau contain rich phosphate deposits that help make Morocco one of the world's largest producers of this mineral. Closer to the mountains, the landscape changes, and there are plains that have especially good soil for farming: the Tadla Plain, located on the Oum Er-Rbia River; the Haouz, at the basin of the Tensift River near Marrakech; the Gharb in the north; Chaouia, near Casablanca; and the Souss Plains, surrounded by the High Atlas and Anti Atlas mountains.

Mountains

Past the plains and plateaus lie the mountain ranges. The northernmost range is the Rif Mountains, which curve in an arc from the Strait of Gibraltar east to the hills of Aith Said. The highest point is Mount Tidirhine at just over 8,000 feet (2,450 m). These almost-impassable mountains, which isolate northern Morocco from the rest of the country, run parallel to the Mediterranean Sea. One natural pass, called the Taza Gap, provides access from the Atlantic through the Rif and the Middle Atlas Mountains; it is the only access route between the Moroccan coast and the rest of North Africa.

To the south of the Rif, the Atlas mountain chain crosses the middle of Morocco from the southwest to the northeast. It contains numerous mineral deposits that include lead, zinc, iron, manganese, phosphates, gold, and silver. There are very few passes through these harsh mountains. The chain is actually three separate mountain ranges: the Middle Atlas (Moyen Atlas) in the northeast, which reach a height of about 10,960 feet (3,340 m); the High Atlas (Haut Atlas) in the central area, which is the tallest range in the country and contains Morocco's highest peak, Jebel Toubkal, at 13,665 feet (4,165 m); and

The foothills of the Atlas Mountains offer farmers fertile land for growing crops.

the Anti Atlas, the lowest of the mountain chains, in the southwest. The entire range extends approximately 1,500 miles (2,414 km).

Desert

The third main geographic region of Morocco, the desert, covers the area south of Agadir on the west coast to Figuig in the east. This boundary marks the beginning of the Sahara Desert, a barren region of sand dunes, rocks, stones, and scattered *oases*. Sebkha Tah, the lowest point in the country at 180 feet (55 m) below sea level, lies south of Tarfaya.

The government of Morocco claims an additional 102,703 square miles (266,000 sq km) of desert territory that stretches to the south along the

Atlantic Ocean. This territory, known as the Western Sahara, is a low, flat desert area with expanses of small rocky or sandy mountains in the south and northeast. It is one of the least populated places in the world. However, many of the people who live there wish to govern themselves; they are represented by a group called the Polisario Front, which resists Morocco's control over the Western Sahara. Neither the United Nations nor the African Union accepts Morocco's claim to the land. The UN has attempted to negotiate a peaceful resolution to the territory's status, but has made little progress in recent years.

Climate

Along its coastal areas, Morocco enjoys a Mediterranean climate, though the Atlantic coast is not as warm as the Mediterranean coast because of the effects of the cool Canary Current. The average temperature in Tangier and Casablanca ranges from 54° Fahrenheit (12° Celsius) in the winter to 77°F (25°C) in the summer.

The weather in the interior is more extreme. In the summer, temperatures in Marrakech, located in central Morocco, exceed 100°F (40°C). When the *sirocco,* a hot wind from the desert, blows across the region, temperatures rise even more. In Fez, to the north, summer temperatures average 81°F (27°C) while winter temperatures drop to around 50°F (10°C). Farther inland, winter days are still hot, with temperatures averaging around 86°F (30°C), but the nights are very cool and sometimes dip below freezing.

In Morocco one may experience the dry heat of the Sahara and the humid, snowy heights of the Atlas Mountains all in one day's travel.

MOORESVILLE PUBLIC LIBRARY
220 WEST HARRISON STREET
MOORESVILLE, INDIANA 46158

Part of Morocco is covered by the sands and rock formations of the Sahara Desert.

Temperatures at the higher elevations often drop below 0°F (-18°C), and mountain peaks are covered with snow for most of the year.

There are two distinct seasons in Morocco: the rainy season in winter and spring (October or November to April or May) and the dry season in summer and early fall (from May or June to September or October). The country experiences almost all of its annual rainfall during rainy season, so during the dry season, serious droughts may occur.

Natural and Man-made Hazards

Geologically, northern Morocco is unstable, and the country is susceptible to earthquakes. The country also experiences droughts. Over the past century, a drought has hit Morocco about one year out of three.

Like much of the developing world, rapid population growth, urbanization, and an absence of strict industrial regulations have led to environmental problems in Morocco. As a result of better health care, sanitation, food resources, and security, Morocco's population increased from 5.8 million in 1921 to about 32 million in 2005. By 2025 the population is projected to surpass 45 million. More than half of Morocco's people live near cities, where most industry is also located. Here, water supplies are often contaminated by raw sewage, and factory emissions frequently make the air unhealthy. In rural areas, overgrazing, drought, and logging have allowed the desert to expand. Annually, the country loses in excess of 61,000 acres (about 25,000 hectares) of forest, which results in widespread soil erosion and thus a reduction of crop yield. Approximately one-third of Morocco's *ecosystems* are damaged.

Much of the architecture in Morocco is ancient. (Opposite) This kasbah, or fortress, is in Dades Valley, sometimes called the "Valley of a Thousand Kasbahs." (Right) The Roman ruins of Volubilis are located near the modern-day city of Meknes. The Triumphal Arch seen here was a site used for military ceremonies.

2 From Dynasties to Independence

MOROCCO'S HISTORY GOES BACK many thousands of years, starting from a time when North Africa was lush and green. From 5000 to 2000 B.C. the grassy Sahara region gradually dried up and became a natural barrier between what was to become Morocco and the southern part of the continent. To escape drought, the people of the Sahara fled first to the Atlas Mountains and then to the coast. Migrants from the Mediterranean and southwest Asia joined them, thus planting the roots of *Berber* civilization. Cave paintings by inhabitants of these early communities still exist in the Anti Atlas Mountains.

Roman Influence

Around 1200 B.C. the Phoenicians ventured from their home in the eastern Mediterranean. They established trading posts and fish-salting operations along the Mediterranean coast of North Africa, including Morocco. The Phoenicians ignored the *indigenous* tribes and poor agricultural lands to the south.

One of the early Phoenician settlements in North Africa grew to become Carthage, which is located in modern-day Tunisia. In the fifth century B.C. the Carthaginians colonized Morocco's northern coast, and during this period, the indigenous inland tribes, called Mauri, established an informal confederation that they called Mauritania.

In 146 B.C. the Romans conquered Carthage, and many Carthaginians fled west to what are now Morocco and Algeria to escape slavery. The victorious Romans soon followed, only to be confronted by the fierce Mauri, whom the Romans labeled barbarians (or Berbers). The Berbers fought the Romans for more than 100 years, but the invaders were able to establish colonies. Gradually, a Berber-Roman civilization began to develop.

In A.D. 40 the Roman emperor Caligula assassinated the Mauritanian leader, Ptolemy. The Mauritanians revolted but were defeated, and their land, which included most of Morocco at the time, became the Roman province of Mauritania Tingitana.

Caligula (A.D. 12–41) was emperor of Rome from 37 to 41, during which time the empire grew to include Morocco.

Mauritania Tingitana was on the outer edge of the Roman Empire. It produced little wealth, as olive oil was the most important export. There is no evidence of a rich cultural life in the area: no writers or poets are remembered, and only one theater has been discovered, in the city of Lixus.

As Roman influence declined, the Vandals moved in to conquer North Africa. The Vandals were a Germanic tribe that had sailed south, taken control of Carthage, and gradually expanded their kingdom.

The Vandals were eventually beaten back and defeated by the Eastern Roman Empire (or Byzantine Empire) in 533. This gave the Byzantines control over North Africa, but they would not hold it for long. Control of Mauritania Tingitana passed from the Byzantine rulers to conquering Arab tribes during the mid-seventh century.

The Coming of Islam

The Arabs brought Islam to North Africa, and for over 1,300 years that religion has dominated the region's culture. Islam is a religion that was first preached by the Prophet Muhammad to the tribes on the Arabian Peninsula. Muhammad united the Arab tribes, and after his death in A.D. 632 the Arabs rode out of the desert to spread the message of Islam.

In 681 Uqba ibn Nafi, the great Muslim hero of the conquest of North Africa, led his troops in a legendary march to the Atlantic Ocean. The invasion was unstoppable, and the general left a series of new towns and cities in his wake. Legend has it that when Uqba ibn Nafi reached the shore, he rode his horse a few steps into the Atlantic and declared that were it not for the ocean, he would continue to conquer lands and convert people to Islam.

Between 705 and 709 Musa ibn-Nusayr, the new Arab governor of North Africa, brought the area of present-day Morocco firmly under Arab rule. In Spain, to the north, deposed Visigoth rulers appealed to Musa for military assistance in order to regain their kingdoms. In 711 Musa sent Tariq ibn Ziyad, a Berber, to Spain with an army of Berber and Arab troops, starting more than seven centuries of Islamic influence in that country.

The Dynastic Period

In 788 a *sharif* named Idris ben Abdallah arrived in the Roman-built city of Volubilis and was made king by the Berber chiefs. His descendents, the Idrisids, would rule for nearly 200 years, until 985. During their rule, they made Morocco a center of Islamic scholarship.

When the Idrisid dynasty collapsed, a series of Berber kingdoms emerged as the rulers of Morocco. The most important of these were the Magrawa (who ruled from 985 to 1070), the Almoravids (1073–1147), the Almohads (1147–1269), and the Marinids (1258–1420). These dynasties resisted foreign invaders, and at various times expanded their power across the Strait of Gibraltar into Europe.

During the 16th and 17th centuries, Morocco experienced a long period of civil war and political instability. In 1659, a sharif named Moulay Rachid gained control of Morocco, ruling until 1672. After his death, his brother Moulay Ismail took over and ruled until 1727. Moulay Ismail was one of Morocco's greatest rulers, expanding the kingdom to include parts of modern-day Algeria and Mauritania. He established the Alawite dynasty,

As the Arabs moved into Morocco, their culture and art began to blend with that of the native Berbers. This doorway arch is typically Moorish in that it includes a horseshoe shape that bends inward toward the bottom.

which continues to rule Morocco today: Mohammed VI, the current king, is the 27th Alawite ruler.

Economic Weakness and Political Instability

During the 19th century, European countries began to claim territory in Africa. France, Britain, and other countries used the labor and natural resources of African colonies to strengthen and enrich themselves. In 1830, France claimed Algeria as a colony. Although Moroccan leaders wanted good relations with the French, they supported Algerian rebels resisting the European invasion. This support ended in 1844, when a treaty was signed that established the border between Morocco and Algeria.

France gradually gained influence over Moroccan affairs. Although Sultan Moulay Hassan I, who ruled from 1873 to 1894, attempted to make governmental and economic reforms, the French were able to prevent changes that threatened their interests in the region. When Hassan died, his 10-year-old son Abdelaziz became sultan, and he invited Europeans to become the main advisors at his court.

By the early 20th century, Morocco was essentially a French colony. France controlled the country's treasury and Sultan Abdelaziz was just a *figurehead*. The 1906 Algeciras Conference, at which diplomats from France, Germany, Britain, Spain, and other European countries agreed that France should control key areas of Morocco's government, angered many Moroccans. The country was facing other problems as well, including widespread famine due to two years of crop failures. On August 6, 1907, Moulay Abdelhafid deposed his younger brother Abdelaziz and became sultan. However, Abdelhafid was no more able to resolve Morocco's problems than his brother had been.

French Protectorate

On May 21, 1911, French troops occupied the city of Fez by claiming to be subduing a civil war. Soon after, the Fez Convention established Morocco as a French protectorate. Protectorates do not, in theory, give up their internal governance to the protector nation. However, Moulay Abdelhafid signed the Treaty of Fez, giving up his right to govern. Under the Treaty of Fez France controlled most of Morocco, while Spain was granted the northern zone and the desert regions of the south.

Representatives from France and Spain sign the Fez treaty in 1912. This treaty established Morocco as a French protectorate, while giving Spain control over Tangier, Rif, Ifni, and Tarfaya.

Morocco was run by French resident general Louis-Hubert-Gonzales Lyautey, who held the post from 1912 to 1925. After Sultan Abdelhafid stepped down from his position, Lyautey chose Abdelhafid's inactive brother, Moulay Yusef, to succeed him. During Moulay Yusef's sultanate (1912–1927), Lyautey restored the peace; modernized the educational, legal, and administrative systems; and developed port cities. Despite these advances, angry Moroccans continued to rebel against European domination.

World War II and its Aftermath

Mohammed V (1909–1961), Moulay Yusef's son, became sultan in 1927. At the outbreak of World War II in 1939, he declared his nation's complete solidarity with the French, and many Moroccans enlisted in the French army. After the war, however, *nationalist* sentiment intensified among Moroccans. The newly created Istiqlal (Independence) Party grew in popularity. Party leaders demanded freedom and independence for Morocco under *Sidi* Mohammed V. The French rejected these demands, but they had popular support, and riots and attacks against French authorities in Morocco increased.

In 1953 the French resident general, Augustin-Leon Guillaume, moved to replace Mohammed V with another sultan, which resulted in riots. When Mohammed V refused to step down, he and his two sons were kicked out of the country. For two years Moroccans expressed anger over the loss of their sultan through terrorism, acts of sabotage, and riots.

As the violence increased, France's resolve waned. On November 16, 1955, Mohammed V returned to a jubilant homeland. On March 2, 1956, the French protectorate officially ended, and Morocco became independent. Spain gave up its claim in the north and ceded Tangier to the new state of Morocco, although the Spanish still maintain *enclaves* in Ceuta and Melilla.

The Challenges of Independence

Independence had been won, but many internal and external problems remained. A war against French rule still raged in neighboring Algeria. And

Morocco had to deal with the draw the recently created state of Israel had on its Jewish population. Many Moroccan Jews sought to emigrate, but the Moroccan government opposed them for political reasons.

In 1958 Morocco joined the Arab League, which had been established in 1945 by seven Arab states: Egypt, Iraq, Lebanon, Saudi Arabia, Syria, Jordan, and Yemen. Under pressure from the League, which opposed the existence of Israel, Morocco made Jewish emigration illegal. In response, Israel began secret efforts to smuggle Jews out. Before the founding of Israel in 1948, around 265,000 Jews had lived in Morocco. By 1967 the country's Jewish community had decreased to approximately 60,000.

Not all of Morocco's initial problems were due to politics. On February 29, 1960, a major earthquake killed approximately 12,000 people in Agadir and destroyed three-fourths of the port city.

On February 26, 1961, the king died. His 31-year-old son, Hassan II, assumed power as both king and prime minister, giving him control over almost all aspects of the government.

Morocco's first constitution was approved by a *referendum* on November 18, 1962, making Hassan II the sovereign ruler. In 1963 Hassan declared a state of emergency when student and worker riots broke out in Casablanca. He lifted the state of emergency in 1970 and introduced a revised, more liberal constitution in 1972. This new constitution made Morocco a constitutional monarchy and increased the number of elected representatives in Parliament. In keeping with his liberal mindset, during the 1970s King Hassan II was one of the first Arab leaders to encourage a political dialogue with Israel. Yitzhak Rabin, the Israeli prime minister, visited

Morocco in 1976. However, in 1979 Hassan began to support Arab demands for Israel to give up territory for a Palestinian homeland, bringing Morocco's policy closer to the positions of other Arab governments.

Morocco and the Western Sahara

When Morocco became independent, it was bordered by the Sahara territory ruled by Spain and by the French colonies of Mauritania and Algeria. Moroccan nationalists argued that the historic Moroccan kingdom had included parts of all of these areas. However, international organizations like the UN and the Organization of African Unity (OAU) rejected this claim. Border boundaries with Algeria remain a touchy issue, but most problematic has been the fate of the Spanish Sahara. Now called the Western Sahara, this sparsely populated desert territory is rich in phosphates and has productive offshore fishing grounds.

In the early 1970s some residents of the Spanish Sahara formed a militant group called the Polisario Front, and began demanding independence for the desert territory. By 1975, the Polisario had gained control over most of the region, and Spain was ready to give up its claim to the Sahara. However, both Morocco and Mauritania claimed *sovereignty* over the Spanish Sahara. The issue went to the UN's International Court of Justice. It ruled that neither Morocco nor Mauritania had a legitimate right to the territory, and that the people of the Spanish Sahara should be allowed to govern themselves.

In an effort to claim the territory, 350,000 unarmed Moroccans participated in what came to be called the Green March on November 6, 1975. As the Moroccans crossed the border, the Spanish army simply departed rather than fire on thousands of unarmed marchers. Later that month, Spanish leaders made a secret deal with Morocco and Mauritania that divided the region between the two countries.

In February 1976, when the Spanish pulled out of the Sahara, the Polisario declared it to be an independent new state, the Saharawi Arab Democratic Republic. However, troops from Mauritania and Morocco soon established order, forcing the Polisario to wage a guerrilla war. In 1979, unwilling to face continued Polisario attacks, Mauritania gave up control over its one-third of the territory. Morocco quickly extended its authority over the entire region in order to prevent a Polisario takeover.

With Libyan and Algerian aid, the Polisario developed into a strong guerrilla force, and it won occasional battles against Morocco's well-equipped troops. But Morocco fought back and eventually built a fortified earthen wall around 80 percent of the territory where most of the Saharawi people lived.

The conflict affected Morocco's political relationships with other countries. Morocco withdrew from the Organization of African Unity when it refused to support the kingdom's claim to the Western Sahara. By 1984 more than 70 nations had recognized the Saharawi Arab Democratic Republic (the civilian wing of the Polisario) as the region's legitimate government, even though its leaders were in exile.

In 1991, Morocco and the Polisario agreed to a cease-fire, and a referendum that would let Saharawis decide for themselves whether they wanted to be part of Morocco or an independent state was scheduled for January 1992. However, the two sides could not agree on the terms of the referendum, and it was postponed several times. Beginning in 2000 American diplomat James Baker, serving as UN special envoy to Western Sahara, presented several plans for the future of the region. Although the Polisario agreed to a 2003 plan that was endorsed by the UN Security Council, Morocco rejected the proposal.

For the next several years, there was no progress toward resolving the status of Western Sahara. Moroccan security forces arrested many Saharawis in the wake of riots during 2005, although the government pardoned 48 Polisario supporters the next year. In February 2007 the Moroccan government presented a new plan to settle the issue. Although Polisario representatives immediately rejected the proposal, political leaders in France, the United States, and other countries said they considered it a fair solution.

Reign of Mohammed VI

King Hassan II died on July 23, 1999, and his son, 35-year-old Sidi Mohammed VI, took over the throne. Known for having a modern vision, his focus has been on educating and finding jobs for unemployed youth and improving conditions for women and the handicapped. In 2003 Morocco's legal system was rewritten to grant greater social rights to women. In 2005 King Mohammed announced that children with non-Moroccan fathers would still be considered Moroccan citizens, meaning that women have the power to transmit legal citizenship.

In addition to progress on women's rights, in recent years Morocco has allocated a large portion of its budget to education. By promoting *vocational* training, the country hopes to attract international investment, improving its

King Mohammed VI celebrates Throne Day at the Royal Palace in 2006. Mohammed VI has been a cautiously progressive force in Morocco, enacting laws in support of women's rights and education.

economy and decreasing unemployment. The government has also been implementing literacy programs, with particular focus on young girls, who have the lowest literacy rate in the country.

Morocco has both a king and a legislature. (Opposite) The Royal Armed Forces parade for their commander-in-chief, King Mohammed VI. (Right) The Moroccan Parliament building is located in Rabat. Mohammed VI has given legislators modestly greater authority, and the parliament has gradually been gaining new legitimacy as a result.

3 A Monarchy Moving Forward

MOROCCO IS A CONSTITUTIONAL MONARCHY with a parliament and, at least officially, an independent judiciary. Under the nation's constitution, the king has ultimate authority. He is commander-in-chief of the Royal Armed Forces and has the power to appoint and dismiss the prime minister and the members of his cabinet. The king may break up the parliament at will. He introduces laws, signs and ratifies treaties, and can pardon accused criminals. The Moroccan constitution also designates the king as the country's spiritual leader, Amir al-Mu'minin (Commander of the Faithful), thus also granting him spiritual authority.

In September 1996 Morocco's constitution was amended by referendum, making the government somewhat more democratic, although the king still retains near-absolute power. A two-chamber parliament was organized. Its upper house, the 270-member Chamber of Advisors, is elected by trade unions, local councils, and professional associations; the 325-member lower house, the Chamber of Representatives, is directly elected by popular vote. Members of the Chamber of Advisors serve for nine years, while members of the Chamber of Representatives serve for five. Parliament now may initiate and approve bills and legislation and establish committees to investigate government matters.

Many of Morocco's current political parties were formed during the French protectorate to work for independence, such as the Istiqlal (Independence) Party and the Parti Democratique pour Independence (Democratic Party for Independence). The Mouvement Populaire (Popular Movement) was created soon after independence, and at least eight other parties have formed since the 1970s.

A year after legislative elections in 1997, a coalition (partnership) government was formed. Hassan II appointed as prime minister the longtime opposition leader Abderrahmane Youssoufi, whose Socialist Union of Popular Forces won the most seats in the elections. Youssoufi's ascent marked the first time in Moroccan history that a partnership of socialist, nationalist, and left-wing parties was chosen to govern—even if they were still under the king's ultimate authority.

Local government in Morocco is organized on three levels. At the top level, governors (appointed by the king) rule the 49 provinces and main urban prefectures. These include four provinces in the Western Sahara. The second level consists of rural districts and municipalities, ruled by *chefs de cercle* (literally, "heads of the circle"). The third level is that of rural communes and

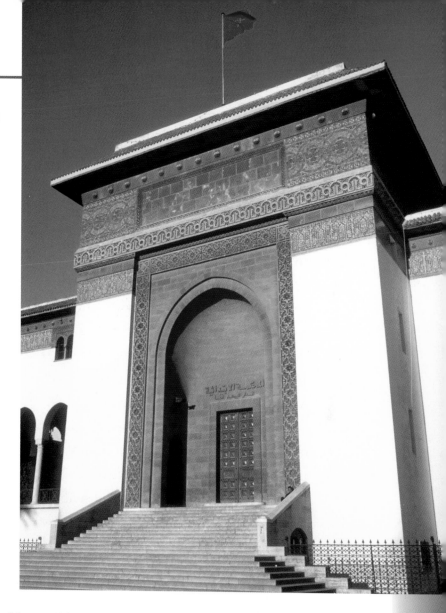

A Berber-style courthouse in Casablanca.

separate urban centers, governed by *qa'ids* and *pashas*. The minister of the interior or the governors appoint the lower-level officials. At each level, a council elected by popular vote decides local issues. The minister of the interior, appointed by the king, has authority over all three levels.

Law and The Courts

The Supreme Court, the highest tribunal in Morocco, sits in the capital city of Rabat and supervises the courts of appeals, regional tribunals, magistrates' courts, and trial courts. The Supreme Court has five chambers: Constitutional, Penal, Administrative, Social, and Civil. The king appoints Supreme Court judges, while judges on the Constitutional Court are appointed jointly by the king and the Chamber of Representatives.

Local tribunals hear cases that involve small amounts of money, up to 300 dirham (equivalent to $33). More important cases are tried in regional tribunals. Above this, there are 15 courts of appeals.

As Morocco is an Islamic state, matters concerning the personal status of Muslims, such as domestic law and inheritance, are referred to *qadis*, Muslim judges who interpret Islamic law. Rabbinical law is applied to personal or religious Jewish questions.

In 1990 Morocco's religious minister proclaimed that Islamic law forbids a woman to exercise political power. The next year, women's groups presented a petition with a million signatures demanding changes to the *Moudawana*, or family code. Traditionally, only men could divorce—and they could do so at will. The petitioners asked that women also be given the right to divorce and that all divorces be handled solely through courts. They also wanted to abolish polygamy (multiple marriage) and to end rules requiring women to have male guardians (*walis*). In 2003 King Mohammed VI enacted reforms that included making polygamy almost impossible (though still legal if the conditions could be met), making divorce an option for both men and women, raising the legal age of marriage to 18 so it was equal for men and women, and giving women the right to their own guardianship unless they choose to hand it over to a man.

Human Rights Reforms

Under King Mohammed VI, Morocco has continued to work on improving its treatment of citizens. The country began improving conditions under King Hassan II when it released long-held political prisoners from secret prisons. Since then, the government has allowed citizens to have a dissenting voice in the political sphere. Notably, newspapers are now able to criticize the government's handling of delicate situations, like the problem of Western Sahara. They can also write articles about sensitive topics like government corruption and violence against women. In 2006, however, the director of *al-Mash`al*, a Moroccan newspaper, was given a suspended prison sentence for printing a story that insulted Algerian president Abdelaziz Bouteflika, so freedom of the press is still a tenuous right in Morocco.

Further reforms have been made to Morocco's criminal justice system. The courts have been altered to allow for appeals based on evidence and not procedural matters. The Supreme Court previously did not review the facts of the case, only whether or not the proper laws were applied.

Perhaps the most progress has been made in the government's willingness to acknowledge and address human rights violations of the past. During King Hassan II's reign, political dissidents often disappeared. Many were secretly arrested, tortured, and held in prisons indefinitely. The government of Morocco long denied that such abuses took place, but under the more liberal government of Mohammed VI, individuals began writing books and telling stories about their experiences. No longer able to deny that disappearances occurred, the government set up the Independent Arbitration Commission for the Compensation of Moral and Material Harm Suffered by Victims of Disappearance and Arbitrary Detention, and by their Beneficiaries. This agency received claims from families and conducted

Morocco's King Hassan II speaks to journalists, 1976. He ruled Morocco from 1961 until his death in 1999. In recent years the Moroccan government has investigated some human-rights abuses that occurred during Hassan's reign.

investigations into supposed human rights violations. In 2003, at the conclusion of the Commission's investigations, 3,700 people received compensation from the government.

Not all developments have been positive, however. In 2003 Casablanca was attacked by terrorist bombers. In response to this attack, the Moroccan legislature passed an anti-terrorism bill that allowed suspects to be held longer without bail and made "the promulgation and dissemination of propaganda or advertisement in support of [terrorism]" a crime. In the weeks that followed the bombing, 2,000 suspects were detained and sometimes tortured. At least one journalist was jailed for publishing letters from Islamists, which the government claimed were justifying the attacks.

Still, Morocco is moving forward in its campaign against disappearances and torture. In 2005 it helped write the International Convention on the Protection of all Persons from Enforced Disappearance. The Convention, which countries may choose to adopt, requires all signatories to pass laws making disappearance a crime. It further requires that the families of those arrested be notified of their whereabouts.

Morocco is home to a variety of industries. (Opposite) Phosphates used in farming to enrich soil are shipped from this facility in Port Safi. (Right) Fishing employs many people in Morocco, and selling fishing rights to other countries provides income for the government.

4 A Vital Economy, But An Uphill Struggle

COMPARED WITH MANY OTHER developing countries, Morocco has a fairly diversified economy. In addition to its traditional core of agriculture, Morocco boasts the world's largest phosphate reserves; productive fisheries; mining, tourist, and light manufacturing industries; and a strong, increasingly deregulated telecommunications sector. Inflation is under control, averaging about 2 percent, a rate comparable to that in some industrialized nations. Over the past decade, however, economic growth in Morocco has been slow, mainly due to recurring drought.

A country's economy is evaluated based on its ***gross domestic product*** (GDP). GDP is the total value of goods and services the nation produces in one year. Morocco's GDP in 2005 stood at more than $138.3 billion, giving the

41

country the world's 56th-largest economy. However, this does not mean that Morocco's people are prosperous. Morocco's Gross National Income (GNI) per capita, a figure that reflects each citizen's share in the country's wealth, was just under $4,400 in 2006, well below the average for North Africa, and nearly one-tenth the GNI per capita of a person living in the United States.

Agriculture

Agriculture employs 40 percent of the workforce and, depending on the harvest, accounts for between 15 and 20 percent of the GDP. Only 20 percent of

The fruit orchards in the Souss plains produce foods that are exported to Europe.

Quick Facts: The Economy of Morocco

Gross domestic product (GDP*):
  $147 billion
Inflation: 2.8%
Natural Resources: phosphates, iron ore, manganese, lead, zinc, fish, salt
Agriculture (13.3% of GDP): wheat, barley, potatoes, sugarcane, olives, citrus, sugar beets, tomatoes, wine grapes, livestock
Industry (31.2% of GDP): phosphate rock mining and processing, food processing, leather goods, textiles, construction, cement
Services (55.5% of GDP): transportation, communications, shipping, tourism
Foreign Trade:
  Exports–$11.72 billion: clothing, fish, inorganic chemicals, transistors, crude minerals, fertilizers (including phosphates), petroleum products, fruits, vegetables
  Imports–$21.22 billion: crude petroleum, textile fabric, telecommunications equipment, wheat, gas and electricity, transistors, plastics
Economic Growth Rate: 6.7%
Currency Exchange Rate: U.S. $1 = 9.04 Moroccan dirhams per US dollar (2006)

*GDP is the total value of goods and services produced in a country annually.
All figures are 2006 estimates.
Source: CIA World Factbook, 2007.

Morocco's land is currently farmable, and more than 90 percent of the arable land relies on rainfall for watering crops, as opposed to irrigation which is more reliable. New irrigation systems are being developed that will provide more than 2.5 million acres (over 1 million hectares) with a reliable supply of water, thus increasing the country's agricultural output.

Morocco is one of only a few Arab nations with the ability to grow enough food to feed its own population, although it chooses to use some of this capacity for cash crops. In an average year, Morocco produces two-thirds of the wheat, barley, and corn that it needs. Citrus fruits and vegetables are exported to Europe, along with dates, grapes, and olives. Morocco is expanding its production of commercial crops like cotton, sugarcane, sugar beets, and sunflowers. Newer crops, such as tea, tobacco, and soybeans, are being cultivated as well, and the wine industry is growing.

However, the threat of droughts, which occur on average every three years, casts a shadow over the country's rich agricultural potential. Droughts in 1999 and 2000 had a destructive impact on Morocco's wheat and barley cultivation. A severe drought in 2005 led to water shortages and affected all sectors of the country's economy.

Commercial Fishing and Forestry

The waters off the coast of Morocco contain several productive fishing areas. An important part of the country's economy, the fishing industry employs about 400,000 people and accounts for more than $600 million in export earnings. The fishing industry, however, lacks the modern fleets and processing plants that would make it competitive with its European neighbors. And periodic fishing bans are necessary to help maintain the country's fisheries.

Morocco renewed its fisheries agreement with the European Union (EU) in 1999. This agreement allows EU countries, particularly Spain, to fish in Moroccan waters in exchange for financial compensation. In the past, Europe has tried to use the fishing agreement as a way to force Morocco to change its internal policies, but in the end the EU deemed the fishing rights more valuable than the possible political gains.

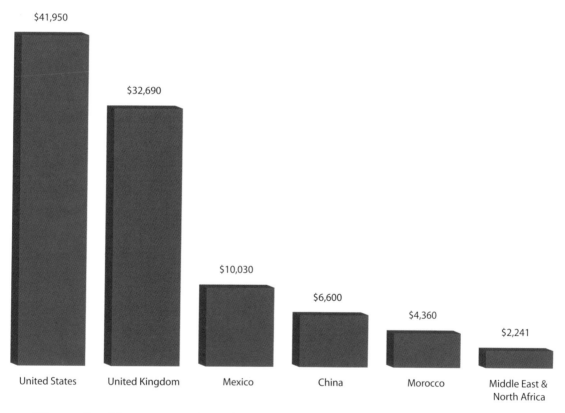

Gross National Income (GNI) Per Capita of Morocco and Other Countries*

Country	GNI Per Capita
United States	$41,950
United Kingdom	$32,690
Mexico	$10,030
China	$6,600
Morocco	$4,360
Middle East & North Africa	$2,241

*Gross national income per capita is the total value of all goods and services produced domestically in a year, supplemented by income received from abroad, divided by midyear population. The above figures take into account fluctuations in currency exchange rates and differences in inflation rates across global economies.

Figures are based on 2005 data. Source: World Bank, 2006.

Morocco's forests are another important natural resource. Forests cover 20 percent of Morocco's total land area. The country meets its own timber needs by harvesting wood from the Middle and High Atlas mountains. The cork and paper pulp from the many cork oak forests are exported to other countries.

Industry

Morocco's industrial sector accounts for 33 percent of the nation's GDP. Major industries include phosphate mining, manufacturing, construction, public works, and energy. Including the Western Sahara territory it is currently occupying, Morocco possesses two-thirds of the world's phosphate reserves. Phosphates are an essential ingredient in plant fertilizers and are also used to make phosphoric acid. Morocco also mines coal, iron ore, copper, silver, and zinc.

The export-oriented manufacturing sector produces construction materials, chemicals, textiles, footwear, processed foods, wines, and petroleum. Artisans create many high-quality leather goods, carpets, ceramics, woodworks, and fabrics that are both sold locally and exported.

The Service Sector

Transportation, commerce, administration, and other components of the service sector employ one-third of Morocco's labor force and produce approximately one-half of the GDP. The country has 24 ports, although Casablanca, one of the largest ports in Africa, handles almost half of all Moroccan imports and exports. Morocco's well-maintained network of roads is one of the best in the continent. It was established during colonial times and has since been expanded. The railway employs more than 13,800 workers and transports people and industrial products on approximately 1,240 miles (2,000 km) of track. Morocco has 11 major airports, which service both trade and tourism.

Tourism also is an important part of the country's economy. Morocco's pleasant climate, excellent beaches, unique architecture, and diverse regions drew nearly 5.5 million visitors in 2006.

Economic Reforms and Challenges

A silver mine in Morocco.

Until 1992 the Moroccan government controlled most of the country's industry. Since then, there has been considerable movement toward privatization (the selling of state-owned enterprises to private investors). By 2005, about two-thirds of the country's state-owned enterprises had been sold, raising over $9.9 billion. The country also implemented a broad range of economic reforms designed to encourage local production. Such changes to Morocco's economy have won the support of the World Bank and the International Monetary Fund.

To develop its economy, Morocco has established several major trade agreements. Morocco's Association Agreement with the European Union

Moroccan stockbrokers use computers to track trades on the country's stock market.

calls for the gradual elimination of tariffs (taxes on imported goods) on Morocco-EU trade in industrial goods until approximately 2012, which should speed up Morocco's economic integration into Europe. The goal of the recent United States North Africa Economic Partnership is to promote the *Maghreb* as a destination for U.S. business and the United States as a market for Moroccan exports. Approximately 30 American franchises, such as Pizza

Hut and McDonald's, have arrived in Morocco, and foreign investment has grown from $50 million to over $2 billion in the past decade.

The government of Morocco continues to face the challenges of high unemployment, payments on its multibillion-dollar debt, and recurring drought. Criticism has been voiced over the slow pace of change, but progress has been made. Mohammed VI has established a commission to improve foreign investment in Morocco, and efforts to liberalize the telecommunications market and other sectors are underway.

Morocco is home to a diverse group of people. (Opposite) Berber women in Imi n'Tanout dress in traditional colorful costumes. (Right) Moroccan Jews pray at the Mellah synagogue in Marrakech. There are approximately 250 Jews still living in Marrakech and perhaps 7,000 in all of Morocco.

5 A Colorful and Dynamic People

MOROCCO'S POPULATION IN 2006 was estimated at 33.2 million—a bit larger than that of the state of California. Nearly half of the people live in cities, and that proportion continues to increase. Overall, Morocco's population is growing slightly faster than that of countries outside of Africa, but the rate is below the average for Middle Eastern countries. More than one-third of the country's population is under 15 years of age.

Religion

Islam is the cornerstone of Morocco's political, spiritual, and traditional social life. The population of Morocco is 98.7 percent Muslim. Most belong to the Sunni sect, Islam's dominant branch. King Mohammed VI is the ultimate spiritual authority in Morocco, empowered to interpret the laws of Islam.

Quick Facts: The People of Morocco

Population: 33,241,259
Ethnic Groups: Arab-Berber, 99.1%; Jewish, 0.2%; other, 0.7%
Age structure:
 0–14 years: 31.6%
 15–64 years: 63.4%
 65 years and over: 5%
Birth rate: 21.98 births / 1,000 population
Infant mortality rate: 40.24 deaths / 1,000 live births
Death rate: 5.58 deaths / 1,000 population
Population growth rate: 1.55%

Life expectancy at birth:
 total population: 70.94 years
 male: 68.62 years
 female: 73.37 years
Total fertility rate: 2.68 children born/woman
Religions: Muslim, 98.7%; Christian, 1.1%; Jewish, 0.2%
Languages: Arabic, Berber dialects, French, Spanish
Literacy: 51.7% (2003 est.)

All figures are 2006 estimates unless otherwise indicated.
Source: Adapted from CIA World Factbook, 2007.

Islamism, or Islamic fundamentalism (a movement to enforce a strict, conservative interpretation of Islam on society and government) is not as strong in Morocco as it is in neighboring Algeria, which causes tension between the two countries. The government takes religious extremism very seriously and does its best to combat the danger of terrorism. Morocco is proud of its tradition of tolerance and works to preserve that heritage.

Only 1.1 percent of Morocco's people are Christians, and of that group most are Roman Catholic. The Christian population in Morocco consists mainly of Frenchmen, Spaniards, and Italians who established roots during different waves of migration and colonization. In 1956 Christians in Morocco numbered about half a million; today the Christian population is approximately 60,000.

Although tiny today (just 0.2 percent of the population), the Jewish community in Morocco has a long history dating back to ancient times. The formation of the State of Israel in 1948 marked a change in that history as the majority of the country's 265,000 Jews moved to the holy land. Today, approximately 7,000 Jews remain in Morocco. Their religious practice combines Berber, Oriental, Arab, and Spanish customs, which distinguishes them from Eastern European Jews.

Growing Up in Moroccan Society

The majority of Moroccans come from Berber communities, but generations of intermarriage with the Arab population and integration into the dominant Arab-Islamic culture have somewhat blurred the differences between Arabs and Berbers. Today, an estimated 40 to 45 percent of the population speaks a Berber language. Of that group, between 75 and 90 percent also speak at least some Arabic. The Berber languages still exist in their original forms, particularly in the mountain regions. French is also common throughout the country. The educated upper class also studies and speaks English. In addition, Spanish is still spoken in the northern areas formerly under Spanish rule and in the Spanish enclaves of Ceuta and Melilla.

Moroccan society is patrilineal (descent is traced through the male line), and male babies are favored over females. Until age two, there is little difference in the treatment of males and females. After that, fathers become more attentive to their sons than their daughters.

Falconry, hunting using birds of prey to catch small animals, is a time-honored tradition in the Arab world and remains popular in Morocco.

In later childhood, between the ages of 6 and 12, girls learn the basics of housework and childcare. At this stage they learn *qul*, more mature behavior, while boys do not acquire this quality until much later (in their early twenties). Between the ages of four and eight, Moroccan boys are circumcised. This is an important religious event.

While girls' status is still not equal to that of boys in Morocco, their value to the family has generally increased as girls have become more educated and begun to engage in work outside the home. Today, some Moroccan women serve as doctors, judges, engineers, scientists, bus drivers, and merchants. The progress of women in Moroccan society has been slow, however. In theory, Moroccan men and women have equal rights in all aspects of marriage and divorce, as well as equal political rights. But in practice the freedom of women continues to be limited in many cases, as Morocco is a Muslim state under Islamic family law that stresses male authority.

Education

Moroccan children are required to attend primary school from age 7 to 13. The government operates primary schools that are open to all. However, the number of students that move on to secondary school drops dramatically.

This is especially true in rural areas, where there are shortages of schools and teachers. In addition, many families require their teenage children to work on the family farms or bring in extra income for the family.

The lack of importance traditionally placed on education, particularly for girls, is reflected in Morocco's literacy rates, which are among the lowest in the Arab world. Only about 52 percent of Moroccan adults can read and write, and there is a wide disparity between men and women. About 64 percent of men are considered literate, compared to just 39 percent of women; in the rural areas the literacy rate for women is estimated at about 10 percent.

Approximately 230,000 students attend Morocco's state universities, including the nation's largest, Mohammed V University in Rabat. The Hassan II Agriculture and Veterinary Institute, also located in Rabat, is known for its social science research as well as its science programs. Located in Ifrane, Al-Akhawayn is Morocco's only private university and has the distinction of being the first English-language university in North Africa. The renowned Qayrawin University in Fez is one of the oldest centers for Islamic study. In addition to these schools, there are numerous technical schools and institutes of higher learning throughout the country.

Housing and Daily Life

In some Moroccan cities, wealthy residents live in large Mediterranean-style villas and modern apartment buildings. Members of the middle class usually reside in more modest attached or semi-attached homes. Many of the country's urban poor live in *bidonvilles*, shantytowns on the outskirts of the cities. *Bidonvilles* developed during colonization when the *medinas*, the original urban centers, could no longer accommodate the increasing waves of people from rural areas. Houses in the rural parts of the country may consist of a single room that serves as a kitchen, living room, bedroom, and barn.

Before European sports were introduced at the end of the 19th century, horsemanship and hunting were the traditional national pastimes. Now, football (what Americans call soccer) is the favorite sport to watch and play. In 1970 Morocco became the first African country to participate in soccer's World Cup. Polo, golf, swimming, and tennis are also popular.

Clothing

In Morocco's past, each style of rural dress represented a tribal identity through fabrics, color, and draping. In urban centers, clothing styles were derived from the Arabic fashions introduced with Islam in the seventh century. Today, traditional clothing is still worn throughout the country, though in cities and towns people often wear Western clothing or a combination of Western and traditional styles. The traditional articles of clothing still worn by men in the city and country include the *jellaba*, a short-sleeved hooded robe; the *selham*, a full cloak with silk pom-poms on the hood; and the *burnoose*, a heavier version of the *jellaba*, often with embroidery around the hood. Many men wear a skullcap or brimless cap. The fez, a hat named for the city of Fez, is red with a flat top and tassel, which is worn for formal events.

When in public, some city women still wear the *haik*, a large piece of woolen or cotton fabric that acts as a hood, cloak, and veil to completely cover the body. Since independence in 1956, however, women also wear the *jellaba* as an outer garment. At home, a long, lightweight robe called a caftan is popular. In the countryside, Berber women weave their own cotton and wool to make the *izar*, a long, flowing piece of draped cloth, and the *hendira*, a blanket-like shawl. Since a resurgence of religious activism beginning in the 1990s, many young, career-oriented women in the cities have chosen to cover their head with a scarf.

Traditional Handicrafts

The arts and crafts of Morocco reflect age-old designs, a rich artistic heritage, and the influences of many great civilizations. In the medina of Fez, there is a leather market where beautiful leather goods can be found. Dark silk embroideries are also sold, and carpenters create finely carved coffee tables, cupboards, and chests.

The king's Royal Guard is dressed in a traditional uniform bearing the colors on Morocco's flag: green, red, and white.

In other quarters coppersmiths sell cauldrons and large trays used for celebrations, and dye merchants display colorful wools, cottons, and silks. In the

The market in Marrakech is the largest in Morocco. Stalls often sell traditional crafts like metalworks, furniture, and baskets.

Andalusian area and the pottery market, beautiful ceramics may be found. In the port city of Essaouira, woodworkers and cabinetmakers create beautiful pieces of furniture and art, and in the town of Tiznit in the south, there is a jewel market as well as stalls where merchants sell colorful traditional clothing. In both urban and rural areas, textile production—namely, weaving and embroidery—is considered Morocco's greatest artistic tradition. Morocco's decorative textiles developed through the centuries into a world-renowned art form.

Rural and urban arts and crafts in Morocco differ in several ways. Urban art objects feature religious symbols and are decorated to celebrate and honor the Islamic religion. In keeping with Islamic law, humans or animals are seldom shown. Although there are regional variations, every craft has its own specific requirements and Arab-Muslim identity that must be maintained.

In rural areas of Morocco, where farming and herding are common, art is *utilitarian*, yet still often beautiful and creative. Rural craft techniques are passed down through families and tribes and are not practiced full-time. Islam plays a smaller role in rural art, and designs tend to focus on nature, including celestial and harvest cycles.

Folklore, Food, and Feasts

Morocco has a deep and expressive tradition of folklore. Cooking, feasts, and celebrations are essentials of Moroccan life, rooted in the culture and character of the people. Generosity and abundance are key aspects of Moroccan hospitality. Meals and *diffas* (banquets) are prepared with an overabundance of food to express a warm welcome.

Some foods one is likely to find at such a feast include bread, which is an important part of every meal, and Morocco's national dish, **couscous**. Couscous is grains of semolina that are steamed over a simmering stew made of vegetables and meat or fish. Three other popular dishes are *mechoui*, an entire lamb rubbed with garlic and ground cumin, then roasted on a spit; *bis-teeya*, a large pigeon or chicken pie; and *djej emshmel*, which is a stew of chicken, lemon, and olives. In the desert and outlying regions, camel, gazelle, hedgehog, and desert fox are part of the nomadic diet, as is a bread made from locusts. Mint tea is also enjoyed in cafés and homes throughout Morocco.

Celebrations, Holidays, and Festivals

Moroccans observe various secular, civic occasions as public holidays. Among the most important are New Year's Day, Throne Day (July 30), the anniversary of the Green March (November 6), and Independence Day (November 18). Yet in a country in which more than 98 percent of the people are Muslim, important Islamic holidays are almost universally celebrated and frequently serve as official public holidays as well.

Moroccan businesses and the government follow the Gregorian, or Western, calendar, but Muslim religious observances are based on the Islamic calendar, which follows the phases of the moon. Because the lunar year is shorter than a solar year, Muslim holidays fall on different days in the Western calendar each year.

Spiritual festivals called *moussems* occur around the same time as religious holidays such as Mawlid (the birthday of Muhammad), Ramadan, and weddings. Celebrated throughout the country, *moussems* praise popular culture, promote commerce, and honor local saints. Every September, in the village of Imilchil in the Atlas Mountains, the Berber marriage *moussem* is held to introduce the semi-nomadic herdsmen to the village women. From early spring to fall, festivals are also held to celebrate the harvest. These lively, colorful events, which occur throughout the country, include the Almond Blossom Festival, Rose Festival, and Horse Festival.

Most Moroccans live in crowded urban areas. (Opposite) The minaret of the Hassan II Mosque towers over Casablanca. The mosque is the second-largest in the world. (Right) The city of Fez is home to about a million people, most of them living in cramped quarters.

6 Cities and Communities

MOROCCO IS HOME to many cities and towns, each with its own style, architecture, and crafts. With an estimated population of 3 million, Casablanca is the country's largest city. The cities of Rabat, Fez, Marrakech, and Meknès, founded as imperial capitals, continue to serve as political, spiritual, and historical centers.

Tangier

A bustling, complex city, Tangier is the gateway to Morocco and is strategically located on the northwest corner of Africa, a few miles across the Strait of Gibraltar from Spain. This city of about 539,000 is closer to Europe than any other major city on the continent of Africa.

The first recorded history begins with the arrival of the Phoenicians, who created a prominent trading port. After the fall of Carthage, Tangier became the capital of the independent kingdom of Mauritania. Later conquerors included the Romans, Vandals, Byzantines, and Visigoths. In A.D. 705 the Arab Muslims conquered Tangier. The Portuguese arrived next, and during the 15th and 16th centuries Tangier was ruled alternately by Portugal, Spain, and then Portugal again. The British were put in control of Tangier in 1662 but departed in 1681.

By 1856 Tangier was the diplomatic capital of Morocco, and by the late 19th century it had become an international trading and diplomatic center. Although many fought for control of the city, the French stayed in power. In 1923, under the Statute of Tangier, the city became an international zone—an unhampered, tax-free open port run by resident diplomatic agents from 10 countries, including Morocco. Soon after the country's independence from France, Tangier again became part of Morocco.

Today, Tangier's economy is based on tourism. King Mohammed VI and his government, along with the European Union, have plans to develop the infrastructure of the city. Government officials have declared their intent to stop the smuggling of illegal drugs and people, which has long plagued the North African port. The U.S. and Moroccan governments attempted to introduce goat herding and beekeeping as legal replacements for cannabis famers but these programs have met with little success.

Rabat and Salé

Rabat, the royal city and capital of Morocco, began as a small settlement and port of call for the Phoenicians and Carthaginians in the third century B.C. In the 10th century, it became a *ribat*, a fortified community of Muslim warriors.

The city flourished in the 12th century, and its sister city on the opposite side of the river, Salé, became the most prosperous harbor in Morocco. In 1912 Resident General Lyautey of France moved Morocco's capital city from Fez to Rabat, where it has remained. Rabat, including Salé, is the second-largest city in Morocco, with a population of about 1.5 million.

Rabat is an orderly, modern urban center where Arabic and European, especially French, cultures coexist. Most Rabatis speak Arabic and French, and some speak Spanish as well. The shallow waters of the Bou Regreg and the prosperous Casablanca harbor to the south have prevented industrial growth in Rabat. However, the city is an important center of carpet and textile manufacturing, fish and fruit processing, and asbestos and brick production. Mohammed V University, the largest university in Morocco, is in Rabat.

In Salé, craftsmen are known for their magnificent baskets and woven floor mats. In the medina, the city's noted *madrassa*, a beautifully restored 14th-century college, is a prime example of Moorish architecture.

Casablanca

Morocco's largest city, Casablanca is a teeming, vibrant metropolis. The city was built on the site of a Berber village that was conquered by the Portuguese in 1575. Portuguese settlers remained until 1755, when an earthquake destroyed their colony. The area never developed into more than a small village until the mid-1800s when the Europeans returned and renamed the town Casablanca. The town began to grow and prosper, but the economic success of the Europeans caused resentment among the local population. Violent

Traffic crowds narrow streets in Casablanca, Morocco's largest city.

uprisings led to the French invasion in 1907 and the eventual declaration of a French protectorate in 1912.

Under French rule Casablanca became an important economic center. Its port was developed, new urban districts were created, railways were expanded, and better roads were laid out. The city's rapid development and promise of prosperity drew many people to Casablanca in search of work. However, unemployment became a problem and *bidonvilles* began to surround the city.

Today, the port of Casablanca is the city's economic center. Covering 445 acres (180 hectares), the port is protected from the Atlantic swell by the long Moulay Joussef Pier. The port of Casablanca is one of the largest in Africa; it handles 37 percent of Morocco's shipping traffic and processes approximately 20 million tons of goods per year. One of the city's striking monuments is the Hassan II Mosque. Completed in 1993, it is among the largest religious buildings in the world, capable of accommodating more than 100,000 people. It also boasts the world's tallest *minaret,* at 689 feet (210 m).

Casablanca is a major transportation hub. Modern highways connect it with other important cities in Morocco. A major railway system travels northeast to Algeria and Tunisia, and international airlines serve the city's Anfa

An electric train departs from Casablanca's Voyageurs Station, the city's main railroad station.

and Novaceur airports. Important industries include textiles, food canning, beer and soft drink production, leather working, and electronics. There is also commercial fishing from the city's coastal waters.

Essaouira

In the seventh century B.C. the small coastal town of Essaouira was a regular stopping point for Phoenician shipping vessels. During Roman times, the

Five gates like this one lead into the medina in Essaouira.

town's scattered offshore islands—the Isles Purpuraires, or Purple Islands—were tapped for their renowned purple dyes. During the Middle Ages the port was a prominent link in the trans-Saharan caravan route. At the close of the 15th century, Portugal seized the small port town, named it Mogador, and built a fort near the water. A few years later, the Sa'adians captured Mogador and Agadir, a coastal town to the south, returning them to Morocco.

In the late 1700s the Alawite sultan Mohammed ben Abdallah had Mogador redesigned to rival the port of Agadir. The new town, renamed Essaouira (meaning "little ramparts"), was laid out on a grid system and surrounded by ramparts. It became an important shipping link between Timbuktu (in present-day Mali) and Europe.

In 1912 the French renamed the city Mogador again, and during the colonial period its commercial role declined. After the French protectorate left, the town—again called Essaouira—became known for its relaxed atmosphere. Today Essaouira, with a population of more than 440,000, is the home of hundreds of craftsmen who use thuya wood to create beautiful goods.

Agadir

Modern, sun-filled Agadir, with a population of more than half a million, is considered the premier seaside resort in Morocco. It is one of the country's most popular tourist destinations. After a devastating earthquake in 1960, Agadir was rebuilt for the tourist trade. The town also boasts one of Morocco's leading fishing ports.

The port of Agadir was established in 1503 by a Portuguese nobleman and was soon sold to the Portuguese government, which developed it into a busy commercial port and hub for caravans. Agadir became the capital of the Souss region—homeland of the Sa'adians, who expelled the Portuguese in 1542. In 1769 Sultan Mohammed ben Abdallah, upset that Agadir had evolved into a rowdy center for military men, sailors, and merchants from across Europe, closed the harbor to European trade and created a rival port in Essaouira.

Fez

Fez is the fourth-largest city in Morocco, with a population of about a million. The oldest of the imperial cities, Fez remains the spiritual center of the country. Originally a Berber town, Idris I founded the present city in A.D. 789, and in 809 his son, Sultan Idris II, declared Fez the capital of the dynasty. Fez was plagued by chaos and famine until it was conquered in 1069 by the Almoravid sultan Yusuf ibn Tashfin. Later it was captured by the Almohads, who ruled in the mid-12th century.

When the Marinids conquered Fez, the city again became the capital of Morocco. During their reign, Fez reached its architectural and intellectual height. A new city called Fez el-Jdid was built in 1276 outside the walls of Fez al-Bali, the old town, as a military settlement and administrative base. Today, Fez al-Bali is among the world's largest thriving medieval cities and has the largest medina in Morocco.

Throughout the 19th century Fez remained the intellectual and spiritual heart of the country. The treaty declaring Morocco a protectorate of France, signed in Fez on March 30, 1912, led to riots in the city's streets. The city became a center of anti-colonialist sentiment and the birthplace of Morocco's Istiqlal Party.

Meknès

The imperial city of Meknès, with a population of 633,000, is perched on a plateau and surrounded by lush plains of wheat, beans, grapes, olives, and citrus. In the 10th century the Zenata Berbers from the Meknassa tribe settled in this fertile region. When Moulay Ismail became sultan in 1672, he made Meknès his capital. Ismail surrounded the city with 16 miles (25 km) of thick walls and began an extensive building program that included his lavish palace. After his death in 1727, the imperial city was left unfinished and the glory of Meknès faded.

Today, the city is a railroad hub and producer of textiles, canned foods, cement, and vegetable oils. Meknès is still surrounded by walls 12 feet (4 m) thick. The main entrance, the Bab el-Mansour, is considered the most exquisite gate in North Africa. The mausoleum of Moulay Ismail is one of the few Moroccan shrines that may be entered by non-Muslims.

Workers dye fabrics and tan leather in these vats in Fez. Textiles and hand-woven fabrics are an important part of the local culture.

The Koutoubia mosque in Marrakech was built in the 12th century. At a height of 221 feet (69 m), it was once the tallest building in Morocco.

Marrakech

Located on the fringes of the desert in the western foothills of the High Atlas Mountains, the imperial city of Marrakech is Morocco's third-largest city, with a population of approximately 1.5 million. Twice it has served as Morocco's capital.

Marrakech was founded in 1062 by the Almoravid sultan Yusuf ibn Tashfin. The extensive development of Marrakech was continued by the sultan's son, Ali, who constructed an elaborate underground irrigation system and a rampart of red earth and stone around the city. The protective wall measured 30 feet (9 m) in height and extended for 5 miles (8 km). The Almohads overthrew the Almoravids and destroyed, then rebuilt, much of the city, including the famous Koutoubia Mosque. Considered one of the most noble and gracefully proportioned mosques in the western Muslim world, Koutoubia features a minaret that soars 221 feet (69 m) into the air. In the 12th and 13th centuries, Marrakech was an important stop for caravans carrying gold, slaves, and ivory from Timbuktu to the Barbary Coast. Marrakech was the capital of Morocco until 1269 and once again the capital under the Sa'adians.

At the beginning of the French protectorate, Governor General Lyautey built a *ville nouvelle* (new city) outside of the old city and worked to restore the ancient medina and monuments. Today, Marrakech is a glamorous city, renowned for its masterpieces of Moorish architecture and the lively Djemma el Fna Square.

A Calendar of Moroccan Festivals

January

January marks the Western celebration of the **New Year**, January 1.

January 11 is the celebration of the Independence Manifesto, which was issued in 1944.

February

The **Almond Tree Blossom Festival** is held in February; the date changes each year based on the blossoming of the flowers. During this time, almond trees are covered in small pink and white buds.

March

On March 2 Morocco commemorates the end of the French protectorate.

April

In April is **Moussem of Aïssaoua**, which celebrates the life of Sheikh Mohammad Ben Aïssa. Members of his religious order dance and sing in his honor.

May

Labor Day is celebrated May 1, as it is in many European countries.

The Rose Festival is held in El Kelaa M'Gouna, usually in early May. There is singing, dancing, and flower-covered floats.

June

Fez hosts the annual **World Sacred Music Festival**, which lasts for a week. Musicians from various religious backgrounds gather to give concerts. They share with others how music helps them connect to God.

July

The **Marrakech Popular Arts Festival** occurs every year in July. The festival celebrates folklore and storytelling.

Throne Day, celebrating the accession of Mohammed VI, is observed on July 30.

August

Allegiance to Oued Eddahab is usually celebrated on August 14, and the **Anniversary of the Revolution of the King and the People** is celebrated on August 20.

The **Celebration of the Young** is celebrated the same day as the birthday of Mohammed VI, on August 21.

September

The **Horse Festival** or **Festival of Fantasia** is usually held in early September. Horsemen get a chance to display their skill as they participate in the pageant.

The Brides' Festival is held in September in the High Atlas Mountains. Potential brides flirt with the gathered men from many tribes and attempt to choose a husband.

October

The Date Festival is held in the Northern town of Erfoud. There are nearly a million date trees growing in the area.

A Calendar of Moroccan Festivals

November

On November 6 the country celebrates the historic Green March into Western Sahara.

November 18 is **Independence Day**, commemorating the return the Mohammed V from his exile.

Muslim Holidays

To determine the dates of their religious celebrations, Muslims follow an ancient lunar calendar that follows the phases of the moon, rather than the earth's journey around the sun. The lunar year is 10 or 11 days shorter than a solar year of 365 days, so according to the Western calendar Muslim holidays shift to different dates each year.

Muharam, the Islamic New Year, is celebrated on the first day of the month of Muharam, the first month in the Islamic lunar calendar. Like the Western New Year's Day, this is a secular, rather than a religious, holiday.

Mawlid al-Nabiy, the commemoration of the birthday of the Prophet Muhammad, is celebrated by prayer and often a procession to the local mosque. Families gather for feasts, often featuring the foods that were reportedly the favorites of Muhammad: dates, grapes, almonds, and honey. The holiday occurs on the 12th of Rabi'-ul-Awwal, the third month in the Islamic lunar calendar.

The **Hajj**—an ritual pilgrimage to Mecca that all Muslims are required to make at least once during their lifetimes, if they are physically and financially able to do so—begins on the eighth day of the month of Dhu al-Hijjah, the last month of the Islamic calendar. On the 10th day of Dhu al-Hijjah, At the end of the Hajj period, Muslims celebrate the festival of **Eid al-Adha**. This commemorates the willingness of the patriarch Abraham to sacrifice his son when asked to do so by Allah.

The ninth month of the Islamic calendar, **Ramadan**, is the holiest period in the Islamic year. During Ramadan, devout Muslims avoid eating and drinking throughout the daylight hours. As soon as the sun goes down, families and friends gather in homes for a meal denoting the end of the fasting day. At the end of Ramadan, Muslims celebrate a major holiday called **Eid al-Fitr**—the Festival of the Breaking of the Fast. This is a joyous time, characterized by feasts and family gatherings; children often receive gifts.

Recipes

Moroccan Chicken

1 can chickpeas/garbanzos
3 lbs. chicken pieces
1 tsp. turmeric
1/2 tsp. ground cumin
salt
1/8 tsp. cayenne pepper
2 tbs. oil
1 large onion, finely chopped
juice of 1 lemon

Directions:
1. Dry chicken pieces with paper towels. Combine turmeric and cumin with 1 tsp. salt and the cayenne pepper and rub into the chicken. Let stand for 15 minutes.
2. Heat oil in a frying pan and brown chicken pieces on all sides. Remove to a plate and add onion to pan. Fry gently until soft, then add garlic and cook a few seconds. Add chickpeas and chicken pieces and 1 tbs. of the lemon juice.
3. Cover and simmer gently until chicken and chickpeas are tender and liquid is considerably reduced (about 1/2 hour). Taste and add salt if necessary. Add more lemon juice to give a pleasant tang.

Moroccan Meatball Stew

Kefta:
1 lb. ground lamb
2 tbs. chopped parsley
1 tbs. chopped fresh coriander
1/2 tsp. ground cumin
1/2 onion, peeled and finely chopped
1/4 tsp. cayenne
salt to taste
2 tbs. olive oil for pan frying

Sauce:
2 cloves garlic, peeled
2 medium onions, peeled and finely chopped
1 green bell pepper, cored, seeded and chopped
1 small bunch of parsley, chopped
2 lbs. tomatoes, chopped
1 tsp. ground cumin
1 tsp. freshly ground black pepper
1/2 tsp. ground cinnamon
2 tbs. fresh lemon juice
1/4 tsp. cayenne
1 1/2 tsp. salt (or to taste)
6 eggs

Directions:
1. Combine all the ingredients for the *kefta* and form into 1-inch balls with wet hands.
2. Heat a 6- to 8-quart saucepan and add the olive oil. Brown the meatballs in the oil, then remove, leaving the oil in the pot. Set the meatballs aside, covered.
3. Add the garlic, onion, and bell pepper to the reserved oil and sauté until the onion is clear.

Add the remaining ingredients for the sauce and simmer, covered, for 30 minutes until the sauce has cooked down to a thick gravy.

4. Return the meatballs to the sauce and simmer uncovered 10 minutes more. Carefully break the eggs into the sauce and poach for a few minutes (don't overcook the eggs). Serve at once.

Moroccan Orange Salad

3 oranges, peeled and sliced crosswise
1/2 cantaloupe, thinly sliced
2 cups carrots, shredded
2 tbs. olive oil
2 tbs. balsamic vinegar
Juice of 1/2 lemon
2 tsp. Dijon mustard
2 tbs. chopped fresh mint

Directions:

1. Divide oranges, cantaloupe, and carrots among 6 salad plates. In a small bowl, whisk together oil, vinegar, lemon juice, mustard, and mint.
2. Drizzle over salads.

Mint Tea

3 heaping tbs. oolong tea (do not use teabags)
2 heaping tbs. dried mint leaves
1/2 cup sugar
water

Directions:

1. Rinse a large teapot. Add tea, mint, and sugar. Pour boiling water into teapot. Cover and let steep for 5 minutes. Test for sweetness, add more sugar if needed.
2. Strain tea into glasses.

Glossary

Berber—a member of any of various peoples that have long inhabited North Africa in the area west of Tripoli, Libya; also the language of these peoples.

bidonville—a shantytown or slum on the outskirts of a city in North Africa.

couscous—the national dish of Morocco, consisting of small grains of steamed semolina.

demarcation—a division into two or more separate and identifiable parts.

ecosystem—a community of organisms and its environment.

enclave—a distinct territorial, cultural, or social unit enclosed within a foreign country.

figurehead—a ruler in name only, lacking any real power or authority.

gross domestic product (GDP)—the total value of goods and services produced in a country in a one-year period.

Islamism—political ideologies based on Muslim fundamentalism that aim at reshaping law and economic policy.

madrassa—a school or college for Islamic studies.

Maghreb—an area that includes the North African countries of Morocco, Algeria, and Tunisia and is often said to include northwest Libya.

medina—the oldest area of a North African city.

minaret—a tall tower attached to a mosque, surrounded by or furnished with one or more balconies from which Muslims are called to prayer.

Moulay—a title given to a Moroccan ruler who is a descendant of the prophet Muhammad or a saint; if the ruler's name is Mohammed, the title Sidi is used.

nationalism—the desire by people who share ethnic and cultural attributes to achieve political independence and a state of their own.

oases—isolated fertile areas in a desert caused by a reliable source of water.

plateau—an elevated area, such as a hill or mountain, with a flat top.

qadi—a judge who administers Islamic law.

referendum—a popular vote for the purpose of deciding a public issue.

sharif—a descendant of Muhammad through the Prophet's daughter Fatima.

Sidi—a title given to a ruler who claims descent from a Muslim saint or from Islam's founder and whose name is also Muhammad or Mohammed.

sirocco—a strong, dry, dusty desert wind.

sovereignty—supreme and independent power or authority in government.

sultan—title given to the ruler of an Islamic state.

utilitarian—designed for practical use rather than for beauty.

vocational—relating to training for a trade or skill to be used in a career.

Project and Report Ideas

Map

Draw a map showing Moroccan cities, rivers, and mountain ranges. Indicate the climate and geography of the regions.

Shopping in Morocco

Research different popular markets in Morocco (Fez, Essaouira, Tiznit). Make a chart, poster, or book and fill it with pictures of the various goods and handicrafts one might find if they were looking for things to buy.

Taking a Vacation

Plan a trip to Morocco. Gather examples of documents you might need (passports, visas, medical certificates, etc.). Prepare your schedule and find or make images that could be used as postcards.

Festivals

There are lots of Moroccan holidays. Research a few and indicate where they are celebrated on a map. See if you can find any pictures of the celebrations.

Project and Report Ideas

The Brides' Festival

The Brides' Festival is based on an old legend. Write out the story in your own words. Compare this story to other famous stories about doomed lovers. In addition, research and report on Moroccan marriage ceremonies.

Write a Biography

Chose a name from the following list of important figures from Moroccan history. Do research to find out about this person and write a one-page biography:

- Idris ibn Abdallah
- Yusif ibn Tashfin
- Moulay Rashid
- Averroës
- Moulay Abdelhafid
- Mohammed V
- Muhammad bin Ibrahim
- Hassan II
- Mohammed VI
- Mohamed Choukri
- Driss Chraïbi

Chronology

ca. 1200 B.C.: Phoenicians arrive on Morocco's northern coast.

500–400 B.C.: Carthaginians arrive in Morocco.

146 B.C.: Romans destroy Carthage during the Third Punic War.

A.D. 60: Berber-Roman civilization begins to flourish in present-day Morocco.

633: A year after the death of Muhammad, Islamic armies emerge from the Arabian Peninsula and begin conquering surrounding lands.

703: Musa ibn-Nusayr claims all of Morocco; Islam begins to spread slowly through Morocco.

788: Idris ben Abdallah establishes the Idrisid dynasty.

1073: The Almoravids gain control over Morocco.

1147: Almoravid control ends and the Almohads take power.

1269: Abu-Yusuf Ya'qub, the first Marinid ruler, captures Marrakech. The Marinids rule Morocco until 1465.

1465: The Wattasid ruling dynasty is established in Morocco.

1525: Sa'adian dynasty begins with Mohammed I.

1644: Moulay Rachid becomes the first Alawite sultan.

1672: Sultan Moulay Ismail begins a reign that lasts until 1727. He constructs Meknès as his capital.

1777: Sidi Mohammed ben Abdallah becomes one of the first heads of state to recognize American independence.

1844: A treaty with France establishes the border between Morocco and Algeria.

1912: The Fez Convention establishes Morocco as a French protectorate and establishes French, Spanish, and international zones.

1927: Mohammed V begins reign, which will last until 1961 (with a two-year exile between 1953 and 1955).

1956: Morocco achieves independence on March 2.

Chronology

1960: An earthquake on February 29 severely damages Agadir, killing about 12,000 people.

1961: King Hassan II begins his reign.

1975: During the Green March, 350,000 Moroccans cross into disputed Spanish (Western) Sahara.

1999: King Hassan II dies on July 23 and is succeeded by his son Sidi Mohammed VI.

2000: Morocco's Association Agreement with the European Union begins; King Mohammed VI makes state visit to the United States.

2002: UN-sponsored referendum in Western Sahara is again postponed.

2003: In May a series of explosions in Casablanca, aimed at Western targets, are linked to Islamic extremists.

2004: The Moroccan government cooperates with Spain in the aftermath of the deadly Madrid bombing in March, in which approximately 200 people are killed. Three Moroccans are arrested in connection with the terrorist attack.

2005: Protestors in the Western Sahara are arrested and jailed despite objections from human rights organizations that their trials were not fair.

2006: The director of *al-Mash`al* newspaper is given a one-year suspended jail sentence for insulting Algerian president Abdelaziz Bouteflika.

2007: The government of Morocco presents a plan for the Western Sahara; Polisario leaders reject the plan in February.

Further Reading/Internet Resources

Boele, Vincent, ed. *Morocco: 5,000 Years of Culture*. London: Lund Humphries Publishers, 2005.

Cassanos, Lynda Cohen. *Morocco*. Philadelphia: Mason Crest, 2004.

Cross, Mary. *Morocco: Sahara to the Sea*. New York: Abbeville Press Publishers, 1995.

Delgado, Kevin. *Morocco*. San Diego: Lucent Books, 2006.

Jereb, James. *Arts and Crafts of Morocco*. San Francisco: Chronicle Books, 1996.

Pennell, C.R. *Morocco Since 1830: A History*. New York: New York University Press, 2001.

Raabe, Emily. *A Primary Source Guide to Morocco*. New York: PowerKids Press, 2006.

Travel Information

http://www.onlymorocco.com
http://www.i-cias.com/morocco/
http://www.lonelyplanet.com/worldguide/destinations/africa/morocco/

History and Geography

http://www.state.gov/p/nea/ci/c2416.htm
http://www.historyworld.net/wrldhis/PlainTextHistories.asp?historyid=ac97
http://www.uam.es/otroscentros/medina/morocco/morgengeo.htm

Economic and Political Information

https://www.cia.gov/cia/publications/factbook/geos/mo.html
http://www.mbendi.co.za/land/af/mo/p0005.htm
http://www.nationmaster.com/country/mo-morocco/eco-economy
http://www.maroc.ma/PortailInst/An/home

Culture and Festivals

http://www.scholars.nus.edu.sg/post/morocco/moroccov.html
http://www.morocco.com/culture/

Publisher's Note: The websites listed on this page were active at the time of publication. The publisher is not responsible for websites that have changed their address or discontinued operation since the date of publication. The publisher reviews and updates the websites each time the book is reprinted.

For More Information

Embassy of the Kingdom of Morocco in the United States
1601 21st Street, NW
Washington, DC 20009
Tel: (202) 462-7979
Fax: (202) 265-0161

Moroccan National Tourist Office
Avenue Allal al Fassi
Madinat al Irfane
Souissi, Rabat, Morocco
Tel: (212) (37)-67-81-00
Fax: (212) (37)-68-67-16
Website: http://www.mincom.gov.ma

Consulate General of the Kingdom of Morocco
10 East 40th Street, 23rd floor
New York, NY 10016
Tel: (212) 758-2625
Fax: (212) 779-7441
Website: http://www.moroccanconsulate.com
Email: info@moroccanconsulate.com

U.S. Embassy in Morocco
2 Avenue de Mohamed El Fassi
Rabat, Morocco
Tel: (212) (37)-76-22-65
Fax: (212) (37)-76-56-61
Website: http://www.usembassy.ma
Email: ircrabat@usembassy.ma

Index

Numbers in ***bold italic*** refer to captions.

Contributors/Picture Credits

Professor Robert I. Rotberg is Director of the Program on Intrastate Conflict and Conflict Resolution at the Kennedy School, Harvard University, and President of the World Peace Foundation. He is the author of a number of books and articles on Africa, including *A Political History of Tropical Africa* and *Ending Autocracy, Enabling Democracy: The Tribulations of Southern Africa.*

Dorothy Kavanaugh is a freelance writer who lives near Philadelphia. She holds a bachelors' degree in elementary education from Bryn Mawr College. Books she has written for young adults include *Religions of Africa* (Mason Crest, 2007).

Page:
2:    © OTTN Publishing
3:    © OTTN Publishing
7:    © OTTN Publishing
8:    IMS Communications, Ltd.
10:   IMS Communications, Ltd.
11:   IMS Communications, Ltd.
14:   IMS Communications, Ltd.
16:   Corbis Images
18:   IMS Communications, Ltd.
19:   IMS Communications, Ltd.
20:   Time Life Pictures/Mansell/
        Time Life Pictures/Getty Images
23:   IMS Communications, Ltd.
25:   Hulton Archive/Getty Images
31:   Chris Jackson/Getty Images
32:   Karim Selmoui/Getty Images
33:   IMS Communications, Ltd.
35:   IMS Communications, Ltd.
38:   AFP/Getty Images
40:   IMS Communications, Ltd.
41:   IMS Communications, Ltd.
42:   IMS Communications, Ltd.
45:   © OTTN Publishing
47:   IMS Communications, Ltd.
48:   IMS Communications, Ltd.
50:   Roger Viollet Collection/Getty Images
51:   Abdelhak Senna/Getty Images
54:   IMS Communications, Ltd.
57:   IMS Communications, Ltd.
58:   IMS Communications, Ltd.
62:   IMS Communications, Ltd.
63:   IMS Communications, Ltd.
66:   Paul A. Souders/Corbis
67:   IMS Communications, Ltd.
68:   IMS Communications, Ltd.
71:   IMS Communications, Ltd.
72:   IMS Communications, Ltd.

Cover photos: iStock (Oleg Seleznev, Lorna Piche, Graeme Purdy, Graham Heywood)
Cover Design by MK Bassett-Harvey, Harding House Publishing Service, Inc.
www.hardinghousepages.com